Child Safety:
How To Talk To Your Kids About Their Personal Safety Without Scaring Them

By:
Gary Martin Hays
Adam Weart
Mary Ellen Fulkus

ISBN: 978-0-9885523-3-3

For more information, please write:
We Published That, L.L.C.
c/o Adam Weart
PO Box 956669
Duluth, GA 30095

Dedication

Within a span of 64 days in 2008, three young women from Georgia or with ties to the state were abducted and murdered. On January 1, 2008, Meredith Emerson was hiking on Blood Mountain in North Georgia with her dog, Ella, when she was abducted, held captive for several days, and then murdered. On March 4th, Lauren Burk, from Marietta, Georgia, was a freshman at Auburn University in Auburn, Alabama. While walking across a dorm parking lot, she was forced into her car at gunpoint, and later shot and killed. Within hours of Burk's abduction, Eve Carson, from Athens, Georgia, was at her home in Chapel Hill, North Carolina where she was attending the University of North Carolina. She was studying when two men broke into the house and took her at gunpoint. A couple of hours later, she was murdered.

The death of these three young women greatly affected me as my wife and I have 3 young daughters. We struggled with what we could do to make sure our girls were safe in this world. Through a mutual friend, I met Viviane Guerchon, the mother of Lauren Burk. I expressed my deep condolences to her over the loss of her daughter. I told her about my daughters and how I wanted them to be in karate classes so they would know how to defend themselves. I'll never forget her response:

> "I think it is good that your daughters know how to defend themselves. I think it is more important that they know how to avoid ever putting themselves in dangerous situations."

This made perfect sense, but I, like so many others, placed the idea of prevention and education lower in importance than that of reacting or responding to dangerous situations. Think about it for a moment: We see child safety organizations pushing "Child ID" kits every day. They tell us if our child is ever abducted, we can identify the body through DNA taken from your kid. This makes NO sense whatsoever! How is this PREVENTING harm from being inflicted on your child?

Viviane Guerchon is the reason I started Keep Georgia Safe. She has made it her goal to see that no other parent would endure the never-ending nightmare she experiences because of Lauren's murder. This book is dedicated to Viviane, and is written in loving memory of Lauren. God Bless you and your family, Vivi, and please know we are pursuing our mission every day to educate our families on how to be safe.

It is also dedicated to the wonderful people that

have supported our mission of Keep Georgia Safe from the very beginning:

- Diena Thompson, Surviving Parent of Somer Thompson
- Mike and Joan Berry, Surviving Parents of Johnia Berry
- Erin Runnion, Surviving Parent of Samantha Runnion
- Elizabeth Smart
- Ed Smart
- Steve Daley, Executive Director of radKIDS, and creator of the radKIDS Personal Empowerment Safety Education Curriculum
- Dr. David Fincher, the faculty and staff at Greater Atlanta Christian School for having the vision to see the importance of preventative education and implementation.
- The attorneys and staff of the Law Offices of Gary Martin Hays & Associates, P.C.
- And my wife, Sheri, and our three daughters, Audrey, Ashleigh, and Ava for their unwavering support of me in this mission

God Bless ALL of you!

Gary Martin Hays

Table Of Contents

WARNING!!!!

IMPORTANT WARNING
ABOUT THE CONTENTS OF THIS BOOK

The material contained in this book **is not** instant protection for your child! We want to make this point perfectly clear. EVEN if you read the material and implement our suggestions with the "What Would You Do Game", this is NOT enough!! NO book can provide the instant, quick fix solution for protecting and empowering your child.

This book is NOT intended to be anything more than a starting point – a beginning for you to start the dialogue with your child (or children) about their personal safety.

So what needs to happen next – after reading and working with your child on this book? It is one thing to *TALK* with your child about their safety, it is another thing to *TRAIN* your child how to keep themselves safe. We strongly suggest you enroll your child in a hands-on personal safety curriculum. And we'll explain why after we give you some information on how kids learn.

Some studies have reported that 20 to 30 percent of the school-aged population remembers what they hear (auditory learning). An estimated 40 percent remember things well when they see it (visual learning). Finally, others learn by actually doing something to help them "internalize the information or skill" (kinesthetic learning). Every child has some primary learning mode or some combination of the three.[1]

The best way for us to teach our children safety is through a program that can incorporate all three of the learning methods – auditory, visual and kinesthetic – so we can train the instinctive brain to kick in for the child if presented with a dangerous situation.

A great illustration for this point can be found in the Spring 2010 Journal of Applied Behavior Analysis. The question was presented as to whether or not children with autism could be taught abduction-prevention skills. The authors write that "[C]hildren with autism may be particularly susceptible to stranger persuasion because of the social deficits inherent in the disorder. For example, they may not discern strangers from known adults, or they may be oversensitive to certain features of abduction lures such as highly preferred items."[2]

In the study, children with autism were taught abduction-prevention skills and other safety concepts using a system known as Behavioral Skills Training, or BST. This is a teaching technique that has been used to teach kids a variety of things, including:

- To avoid consuming poisons;[3]
- To behave appropriately after discovering a gun or other firearm;[4]
- And even to resist complying with a stranger's abduction tricks;[5]

BST consists of four (4) elements:

1. Instructions: The child is told what to do.
2. Modeling: The child is shown what to do.
3. Rehearsal: The child practices the instructed and demonstrated response.
4. Feedback: The child is given corrective instructions, if needed, and praise as they perform the technique.

The children in the study were taught the following abduction-prevention responses:

1. To say "NO" when someone they did not know came up to them with an abduction trick, such as "I lost my puppy. Can you help me find him?"
2. To immediately run from the area to a safe place;
3. To immediately tell a trusted adult about the person and what happened.

BST is a very effective method of teaching and reinforcing safety concepts, and should be an integral part of any safety training course. Again, we want to reinforce this extremely important point: It is not enough just to talk to your kids about their personal safety. We encourage you to actively seek out a program that addresses safety issues, and then reinforces appropriate responses to dangerous situations through skills and drills.

I. Introduction

Child safety. Who can argue with this as a goal for any organization? It is certainly not a controversial objective. Since 2008, it has been the mission of our non-profit, Keep Georgia Safe, to educate families on how to be safe. But it is very interesting to see the *reactions* we get from parents when we broach the subject of child safety.

We normally get one of three different responses. Let's look at these responses in more detail.

(1) "I don't want to hear about it."

This is the "stick your head in the sand and pretend the problem doesn't exist approach." No parent wants to ever consider something bad happening to his or her child. The thought of a child - *their* child - being the victim of an abduction or a sexual assault is too much to handle. Instead of facing the realities that bad things can happen, these parents cover their ears and walk away.
When you think about it - it is easy to understand why there is an aversion. This paralyzing fear is further fueled by the different scenarios that are covered on a daily basis on the television news programs:

- The child that is abducted while walking home from school.
- The teenage bullying victim that commits suicide.
- The little league coach who is arrested for sexually assaulting players.

With headlines like these, why would any parent want to watch the news or read a paper?

But think about this for a moment: Are we doing our children any favors by ignoring that problems do exist in our world? Are we putting them at risk by not doing all we can to educate ourselves - and them - on how to be safe?

John Walsh is the surviving parent of Adam Walsh, a young boy that was abducted from a mall in Hollywood, Florida, and murdered in 1981. Most of us know John as the creator and host of the television series **America's Most Wanted**. Since Adam's abduction, John has been a leading advocate of child safety initiatives.

On the HBO program "How To Raise A Street Smart Kid," released in 1987, John said "To put your head in the sand, to bury your head in the sand and say my child could not be victimized, in light of all the things that have happened in this country and what continues to happen, is doing your child a disservice. It's tough stuff. But you've got to remember your child is the potential victim. You won't be the victim."

Gavin De Becker, author of "Protecting The Gift", adds another perspective to this. In order to protect our kids, we must first know how to recognize danger and protect ourselves. It is very clear that "[s]afety for children is a matter of safety for parents first. Much as an adult airline passenger is advised to put on her own oxygen mask before putting one on a child, a mother must be safe in order to protect a child. Sacrificing her safety or peace of mind does not add to her child's safety or peace of mind. It isn't either/or - it's both."[1]

(2) **"There is no way that could happen to my child."**

Some parents will try to assure themselves this could never happen to their child. They will try to convince themselves:

"These "predators" do not live in my neighborhood."

We can't get in the mindset that our neighborhoods are completely safe. The U.S. Department of Justices estimates there is one registered sex offender per square mile in the United States. The sex offender could be your neighbor! Even gated communities can give you a false sense of security. We may think the guards at the gate will screen the people coming and going into the community. But they are not doing criminal background searches on these visitors to the neighborhood. The security guard does not know whether or not

My body belongs to me

$ 649.65 M4

Oh I'd say 4 - how total to tell to your
kids about...
Hanzbury.

362 36 #4

→ Brenden Coen

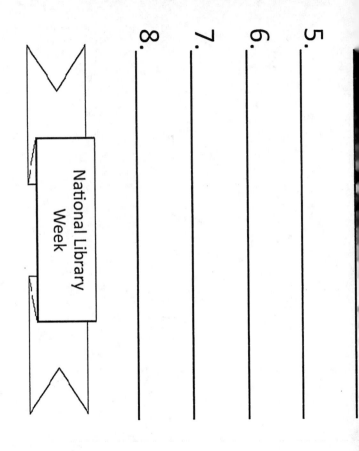

National Library
Week

5.

6.

7.

8.

the person is a registered sex offender or has a violent past. They are just making sure they are on "the list" to gain access to the neighborhood - to cut a lawn, to service an appliance, to unclog a toilet. Their reason for being there may be legitimate. However, what they may be tempted to do while in the neighborhood could be very sinister.

A "2006 Update to the Washington State Attorney General's Report: Investigative Case Management for Missing Children Homicides"[2] gives us some startling statistics. The initial study reviewed a total of 577 abduction cases from 44 states between 1993-1997. Another 175 cases were added in the 2006 update. It found:

- In most cases, the initial contact between the victim and the killer was within 1/4 mile of the victim's residence.
- Most victims (80%) were abducted within 1/4 mile of their last known location.
- 66% of the killers were at the abduction site for a legitimate reason (Think about the number of work vans traveling through your neighborhood for legitimate reasons).
- 29% lived in the area. (Remember: on average 1 registered sex offender per square mile in the US. Is it your neighbor?)
- And why did the killer select that child as the victim? 57% of the abductions were crimes of opportunity!

-"My children are too young to be exposed to threats from sexual predators."

Think again. De Becker further writes in Protecting The Gift that "[t]he most common age at which sexual abuse begins is age 3." Another study by Debra Boyer and David Fine found that 24 percent of female child sexual abuse survivors were first abused at age 5 or younger.[3]

-"I never leave my child alone with strangers."

Please do not believe this practice protects your child! "Approximately 60% of boys and 80% of girls who are sexually victimized are abused by someone known to the child or to the child's family.[4] This is a very chilling thought - that parents need to check out their friends and family members first. But this is an extremely important point for parents - be very careful about who you allow to have unlimited access to your child.

Let's illustrate this point further with a question for parents of boys between the ages of 10 and 18. Would you entrust your son to an organization that allegedly:

- "Failed to report hundreds of alleged child molesters to police and often hid the allegations from parents and the public."
- Kept a comprehensive "blacklist of alleged molesters" dating back to 1919 in internal "perversion files."
- "Frequently urged admitted offenders to quietly resign - and helped many cover their tracks."[5]

What if you were told this organization happened to be the Boy Scouts of America? These frightening details were reported on September 16, 2012 in an article that appeared in the Los Angeles Times after the authors reviewed 1,600 files between 1970 and 1991. Approximately 80% of the time, the authors found "no record of Scouting officials reporting the allegations to police." Even

worse, in over 100 cases, officials "actively sought to conceal the alleged abuse or allowed the suspects to hide it."
Revelations like this make you question whether or not you will ever entrust your child to anyone's care!

(3) "Thank you for telling me how I can keep my children safe!"

We love this response and we hope this is how you will feel after reading this book. Ignorance about violence in our world does not increase the likelihood that you - or your family - will remain safe; nor does denial - refusing to admit that we can be victims if we are not careful. In our opinion, education is the key.

We want to be with our children 24 hours a day, 7 days a week to help keep them safe in this world. We want to put our kids in protective headgear, knee pads, and bubble wrap every time they walk out the door. But author Anne Cassidy writes in her book, Parents Who Think Too Much, "[T]he suits of armor we provide them are as dangerous as the world we're protecting them from."[6] We can not become so obsessed with our children's safety that our worry becomes debilitating paranoia.

There has to be a balance for you, as the parent, and for your child. The last thing you want to have happen is to have your child fear that the boogey man is hiding in the closet or behind every bush. You also do not want to ruin that childlike innocence.

So what can you - as a parent - do to teach your child about their safety without scaring the daylights out of them?

We are glad you asked as we have some very practical suggestions for you! We are going to show you how you can start the dialogue with your child or children to cover a variety of safety topics - ranging from abduction safety to bullying to internet safety to out and about safety. We think the most important thing you can do right now - especially if you have never done it before - is to start the conversation about safety with your children.

We will tell you in detail how you can use a simple game called the "What Would You Do" game to broach some very serious subjects with your children in a way that should not make them feel scared or frightened in any way. The beauty of this game is that it does not have 1000 little plastic parts that your kids can lose in the carpet or under the sofa. There is no game board nor any reason to keep score. It can be played at any time.

And please don't tell us "I really just don't have time for this" - because you do! Think about it. How much time do you spend in the car with your kids - driving them to and from school, or ballet, or football practice? If you are anything like any of us, a lot of your time is spent as a "taxi service". Please turn off the radio, stop playing the movie on the car's video system, and play the game. Or you can play it while you are around the dinner table or at a restaurant. This is great quality time - family time - and such an important discussion that you do not want to wait another day.

We will tell you more about the game later. But first let's talk about your family's safety.

II. Should We Be Concerned About Our Family's Safety?

Crime occurs every day in all communities. It does not discriminate based on sex, race, or socioeconomic status. We see it in pretty graphic detail when we turn on the television. We read about it when we pick up the newspaper and we hear about it when we turn on the radio. If our kids walk into the room, we quickly reach for the remote to change the channel and hope and pray they did not hear or see the violence. Your child asks you why you changed the channel and you simply respond that you wanted to see what else was on tv.

We know crime exists. But when it comes to our family - to our children - we never like to consider the possibility that something could happen to them. Is ignoring the problem really going to protect you and your family? Do you still think the world hasn't changed since you were a kid? Remember those days? Your parents would leave the doors unlocked at night and the windows open to allow the fresh air to gently blow through the home. This was a time when no one would have ever thought about installing an alarm in their own home. We didn't know about mace or Tasers or carjacking. The bicycle was our method of transportation as we would ride it most anywhere at any time and never think twice about it.

But like it or not - times have changed . . .

There is nothing like the innocence of a child. They think the world is a beautiful place. Why would anyone want to hurt anyone else - especially them? As a parent, we always have concerns for their safety and well-being. But we don't want to alarm them or over-react. We also don't want to destroy their innocence or paralyze them with fear.

So we revert back to denying the problem exists. It could never happen to me or my family. Things like this always happen to someone else. " I know how to be safe", and we re-assure ourselves " I never leave my children alone." We are comforted when we remember that they understand the whole "stranger - danger" concept. We reach for the remote, sit back on the couch, and turn the TV to our favorite reality show.

But let me give you a few disturbing facts about crime, and then you can answer whether or not you are worried about your family's safety:

> According to the Federal Bureau of Investigation's Uniform Crime Reporting Statistics Database that profiles the number of reported indexed crimes, in 2011 there were 1,203,564 violent crimes:

2011 REPORTED
INDEXED VIOLENT CRIMES

Aggravated Assaults - 751,131

Robberies - 354,396

Forcible Rape - 83,425

Murder - 14,612

There were also 2,188,005 Burglaries

Does that get your attention?

So we know there is a problem. We realize our children are vulnerable. We know we are at risk. What do we do to protect ourselves and our families from being a statistic?

We believe knowledge is the ultimate defense. If we do not know **HOW** to avoid a dangerous situation, or recognize **WHEN** we are in a dangerous situation, then we are very vulnerable to having bad things happen. Educating ourselves and our family on how to be safe is vitally important.

So what are schools doing now to educate our children on how to be safe?

III. The "Once A Year Safety Day Program" In Our Schools

This is by no means an indictment of our teachers. Mary Ellen is a former teacher and all of us agree they are underpaid and under-appreciated. But in our opinion, our schools are not doing a good job of teaching our kids how to be safe.

Let's explain this in more detail:

Many schools have been conducting their "Once A Year Safety Day Program". All the kids and teachers are gathered together in the school gymnasium for a one hour assembly on how to be safe. Topics include subjects such as fighting in school, bullying, fire safety (including a chance to see a fire truck), and school bus safety.

But there are some problems with this approach:

(1)   What happens if your child happens to miss this program?

Best of luck to that kid until next year?

(2)   What is being "lectured" at these safety seminars - Stranger Danger?

We need to stop this particular safety tip - "Stranger Danger" - right now as it is truly confusing to our children and sends so many wrong messages. This is "old school" safety advice.

Just who is a "stranger" to our children? Ask them, and we bet they will say something like this:

- "He is scary looking."
- "He wears sunglasses and has a beard."
- "He is missing a lot of teeth."
- "He looks like he needs a bath."
- "He smells funny."

- "He wears a mask."

A child's definition of a "stranger" does not include someone who is nice looking, smiling, or friendly. Predators know this. They work at being nice, friendly, trustworthy, and likeable so they can groom and disarm our children and get them to lower their protective barriers and instincts.

(3)   Do our kids really LEARN anything when we try to TALK to them about safety? In other words, is there a better way for them to learn?

Think about Charlie Brown's teacher for a moment. "Waah waah woh waah waah". Is this what our kids are hearing in a safety assembly. The kids sitting around them are not really paying attention, and others are giggling at the class clown making funny faces. The message goes in one ear and out the other. The kids are not engaged in any aspect of the presentation so nothing is really going to be remembered.

Is there a better way to TEACH our kids about safety? There is, but we want to stress the dialogue should first start at home. And we shall show you how . . .

IV. Playing The "WHAT WOULD YOU DO?" Game

How do we keep our children from becoming victims?

Education is the key. And it starts with a simple conversation between you and your child.

We need to make sure our kids are taught to:

1. Understand and be able to recognize dangerous situations and behaviors.

2. Trust their gut - to trust their instincts. If something does not feel right to them, it probably isn't.

3. Have the self-confidence to be able to say "NO" if they ever feel threatened.

By about the age of three, you can start teaching your child some simple safety rules or concepts. But remember: each child's ability to comprehend and practice safety is affected by their age, maturity, and developmental level. Also know this is a gradual process that will not happen overnight and it will require reinforcement from you.

A great way for you to work on your child's self-protective instincts is to rehearse safety situations with him or her. We suggest you turn these safety scenarios into a game that can be fun, interactive, and non-threatening.

We call this the "What Would You Do" game. It is great for kids in our day and age that are used to being entertained. Most kids will escape to the "I'm not listening" mode if they think you are lecturing them. This game is easy and convenient for you to do as well. You can play the game while you are in the car driving to school, going to soccer practice, or at the dinner table.

How do you play the "What Would You Do?" game?

You create a safety scenario that provides a real-life situation for your child so your child can respond and you can discuss possible answers. Make sure you let your child answer each question. Give them time to respond. The goal is to hear their thoughts before you give them the answer. It is better that you allow your child to give you their answer - even if it is the wrong answer.

You want to hear that wrong answer now so you can correct it, rather than to have them make a mistake in the real world. This will give you an opportunity to correct their mistakes, and praise them when they give you the right answer.

In the next chapter, we give you several safety scenarios that you can discuss with your kids. We include a suggested initial question that you can ask for each topic. We also have some follow up questions you can use. Feel free to use your own too. But please notice that none of the questions are too specific and are somewhat void of details. For example, if you asked your child the following question:

> "What would you do if you were walking down the street in our neighborhood and an old man with a beard wearing a baseball cap in a black van pulled over and asked you to help him find his lost puppy?"

The problem with this scenario is that it may teach your child to fear:

- Old men
- Men with beards
- Men wearing baseball caps
- Black vans

We also have a section that will give you lessons that your child should take away from that particular discussion. There is also a final section that provides notes for parents, grandparents, or care-givers about the safety subject.

V. Safety Scenarios

Safety Topic: Child Lures (Lost Puppy Trick)

What would you do if:
What would you do if you are outside playing by yourself and a grownup asks you to please help them find their lost puppy?

Questions:
1. What if this person instead asks you to help find a lost kitten?
2. What if you have seen this person before, but don't really know them?
3. What if this person has a picture of their missing pet?
4. What if the person asking for help is a woman?
5. What if your brother or sister is with you at the time?
6. What if the person offers you a special reward, maybe candy or a toy, for helping them find their lost puppy?

Lessons your child should learn:
Children need to learn that unfortunately there are good and bad people in this world. Instead of teaching "stranger danger", teach your child to judge if a person is good or bad by their actions, not

based on how they look.[1] Make sure your child understands that they are not required to help or assist any adult that asks! Explain that adults can always find another adult to help them. Stress to your child that if an adult they do not know asks them for help, it may be a lure or trick.

Notes for Parents:
Teach your children to run away from danger and requests from adults they do not know. Practice by role playing with your child. Make sure you give your child permission to say "No!" to an adult. Remind them that they should NEVER go off with any adults they do not know and to yell, scream, fight and kick if anyone tries to grab them. Provide a demonstration on resisting with your child and have them practice. Reassure your child that you are the BEST pet detective. If anyone approaches them about a lost dog or cat, they should quickly run away to a safe place and find you or another trusted adult.

Safety Topic: **Out and About**

What would you do if:
What would you do if you were walking down the street and a person driving in a car slowed down to talk to you?

Questions:
1. What if you believe this person may be lost?
2. What if they offer you a ride?
3. What if they offer you ice cream or candy?
4. What if they tell you to get into the car?
5. What if they are in a brand new, cool sports car?

Lessons your child should learn:
Children should never approach a person in a car that stops or slows down when they are out and about. Teach your child to NEVER get into a vehicle with someone they do not know. Explain and demonstrate how fast your child should run away and how loud they should yell in the event someone in a car tries to persuade them to come closer. Ensure your child knows that if a person in a car needs directions or help, it is not their responsibility to help them. The person in the car should ask another adult for assistance instead of a child.

Notes for Parents:

Make sure your children understand the importance of staying away from persons driving in cars, trucks, vans or any vehicle that tries to approach them. Give them permission to yell loudly "No!" and run away. Stress the importance of the "buddy" system with your child. Ensure children are receiving proper supervision. A visible adult who is watching the children serves as a good deterrent for those who may want to harm children. Encourage and help your child develop their "own" method for when they feel threatened or scared and need to run to a safe place or person for help. Review and practice the strategy with your child.

Safety Topic: **Parking Lot**

What would you do if:
What would you do if you are in a parking lot and there is a man nearby asking for money?

Questions:
1. What if you just happen to have a dollar on you?
2. What if he is holding a sign stating the need for gas money?
3. What if you frequently discuss helping others at your church or temple?
4. What if this person approaches you?
5. What if it is cold outside?

Lessons your child should learn:
By nature, children want to help and please others, especially adults. However, it is not safe to approach persons in parking lots who may be asking for money or who even may want to try and steal valuables. Remind your child that it is not their responsibility to help adults,[2] even homeless adults, when they are out in public. Instead, teach your children to keep a safe distance from panhandlers and to walk or run the other way. Further explain to your child that the best way to help these people is to volunteer or support organizations dedicated to providing assistance for the homeless and less fortunate.

<u>Notes for Parents:</u>
We strongly believe that the "buddy system" does not just apply to swimming pool safety – the idea of never swimming alone, but always swimming with a buddy. This also applies any time you and your child are out and about. There is safety in numbers. Your child should never be alone in a parking lot. "Role play" this scenario with your child and help them identify routes to safety. Have your child practice saying "No!" and quickly getting away. Explain the dangers of alcohol and illegal drug addiction to your child and point out that some homeless people beg for money in order to buy alcohol and drugs. If your child would like to help the homeless, contact a local shelter and ask what kind of supplies or food donations are needed.

Safety Topic: **Abduction Prevention**

What would you do if:

What would you do if a grownup you do not know grabs your arm and tells you to come with them?

Questions:

1. What if this person is a female?
2. What if this person tells you that your parents sent them to get you?
3. What if this person will not let go of you?
4. What if you are in a store when this happens?
5. What if you believe this person may live in your neighborhood?

Lessons your child should learn:

Ensure your children understand that they are not to go off with anyone they do not know! Teach them to yell, scream, kick, bite and resist in every manner to get away and run to a safe place. Children need to know that they are more precious and more valuable than any object![3] If something like this were to occur in a store, public park, near their school or in their own neighborhood children should resist by yelling loudly and trying to break free, and then run to a safe place.

Notes for Parents:

Teach your child to yell "You are not my Dadddy/Mommy!" and to kick and scream and resist in every manner possible. Tell your child that they are not to go with this person under any circumstances! Give your child permission to kick this person in the groin, hit this person in the nose, strike this person in the eyeballs, and to bite this person. Find a safe way to demonstrate this with your child. Have your child practice running away to a safe location and/or person and calling emergency numbers or 911 for help. Revisit and practice with your child. Children learn best through repetition and reinforcement.

Safety Topic: **School Bus**

What would you do if:
What would you do if another child's parent showed up at your
school bus stop and told you to come with them?

Questions:
1. What if you thought this parent was nice?
2. What if your own parents did not give you permission to go with
this person?
3. What if it was raining outside?
4. What if the parent was alone?
5. What if your parents do not know this person?
6. What if someone threatens you at the school bus stop?
7. What if you are threatened while you are riding on the bus?

Lessons your child should learn:
Make sure your parents know where you are at all times and always
contact them before a change of plans. Do not accept rides from
anyone unless you have prior permission from your parents. While
waiting at the bus stop make sure you stand far away from the road
and traffic.

<u>Notes for Parents:</u>
Teach your children to regularly check-in with you about their whereabouts and plans. Discuss the adults in your child's life that they can trust. Give them permission to say "no" to an adult and to always trust their instincts. Help your child identify safe places and safe people to whom they can go to if they are ever frightened, scared or need help. Have your child review and practice their "own" method for staying safe with you. We always suggest you or another trusted adult go with your child to the bus stop and wait for them to load the bus before leaving.

This also applies when they are returning from school – wait for them at the bus stop.
A report issued by the National Center for Missing & Exploited Children (NCMEC) on August 30, 2012, concluded that our children are at a great risk of abduction when going to and from school and other school-related activities. The analysis shows "that approximately 35 percent of attempted abductions of children occurred when the child was going to and from school or school related activities." Take away that crime of opportunity by being there with your child.

Safety Topic: Bullying

What would you do if:

What would you do if you were trapped in the bathroom with a bully?

Questions:

1. What if the bully made threats against you before?
2. What if the bully demanded money or something from you?
3. What if the bully was calling you names and teasing you?
4. What if you had previously witnessed the bully picking on other students?
5. What if you were worried you would get into trouble with the school or your parents?

Lessons your child should learn:

Children need to fully understand that no one is ever allowed to inflict harm upon them![4] Encourage your child to stand-up for themselves and to say firmly and loudly "stop, no, you don't get to hurt me" and run out of the bathroom. The child should immediately report the incident to a trusted teacher or adult. Children should not feel embarrassed or ashamed about telling. Remind your child that they will not be made to blame if someone is trying to harm them- it is best to ALWAYS tell.

<u>Notes for Parents:</u>
Make sure that your child knows it is OK and legal for them to defend themselves against a bullying attack, and then run away. It is not OK to "finish the fight" and to strike back repeatedly.
Encourage your child to be an active bystander by reporting teasing and bullying and to speak out against it. Ask your child to always come to you if anyone is trying to hurt them. Reassure your child that sometimes everyone needs help, and some problems are too big for one person.

Safety Topic: Good/Bad/Unwanted Touch

What would you do if:
What would you do if a trusted adult gave you a quick hug for a job well done?

Questions:
1. What if the hug made you feel icky inside?
2. What if you were completely OK with the hug?
3. What if a trusted adult asked you to keep a secret from your parents?
4. What if someone asked you to show them your private parts (parts covered by a bathing suit)?
5. What if someone asked you if they could touch your private parts?
6. What if they tried to touch your private parts?

Lessons your child should learn:
Explain to your child that there are good, bad and unwanted touches. Good touches do not hurt or make us feel uncomfortable. Bad touches hurt. Unwanted touches make you feel uncomfortable or "icky" inside. Some children may be OK with a hug or pat for a job well done, and some children may not like it. Your child is the one who determines what is good or bad. Make sure they understand that "their body" is "their body alone" and no one else's. Give them permission to tell an adult "No!" Tell your children to always come to you or a trusted adult if anyone tries to hurt them or trick them. Ensure they understand that they will not be blamed, and will never have to take responsibility for someone else's actions!

Notes for Parents:
According to The National Center for Missing and Exploited Children, 1 in 5 girls and 1 in 10 boys will be sexually victimized before the age of 18. Ensure your child knows that no one has the right to touch or hurt their private parts (parts covered by a bathing suit). Teach them that if anyone should ever try to touch or hurt their private parts to yell "NO!" and run away from this person. They will never be blamed for the bad actions of another person, or if anyone

is trying to trick them or hurt them. It is their right to always tell! Encourage your child to always come to you if anything is bothering them. Listen to them and try not to become angry or mad. If you do get upset at whatever they are telling you, be sure you communicate to the child that you are mad at the other person for hurting or tricking them, not your child.

Safety Topic: Sexual Assault Prevention

What would you do if:
What would you do if someone tries to hurt you or your private parts?

Questions:
1. What if this person is a family member?
2. What if this person is someone you know or someone we know?
3. What if you are scared this person will get you into trouble?
4. What if this person goes to your school?
5. What if this person asks you to keep it a secret?
6. What if this person threatens you or our family if you tell us what they did (or tried to do?)

Lessons your child should learn:
First and foremost, children need to understand and take to heart that NO ONE is ever allowed to harm or hurt them. They can say "NO!" yell for help, run away, and tell and parent or trusted adult. Further explain that they should always tell if someone is trying to hurt them or make them feel bad inside. They will never be blamed and the person trying to hurt them should be punished! It is important to tell on this person so they will not try to hurt or trick other kids.

Notes for Parents:
Have your child practice yelling "NO!" and running to a safe place to call 911. Discuss safe places and persons your child can go to if they need help. Make sure your child knows and feels that they are one of a kind and very important. No one is ever allowed to harm or hurt them![5] Encourage your child to always trust their instincts and to act on them. Communicate to your child that you will never be mad or ashamed of them if someone tries to trick them or hurt them. Ask them to come to you anytime for any reason if they are scared, confused or need help.   Reassure them that "no matter what" you will always be there for them!

Safety Topic: Home

What would you do if:
What would you do if you are home alone and someone knocks at your front door?

Questions:
1. What if it is a neighbor?
2. What if it is a delivery person?
3. What if you do not know who this person is?
4. What if your parents will be home soon?
5. What if the person tells you to open the door?

Lessons your child should learn:
Your child should not open the door to anyone when they are home alone unless they have previous permission from you. If the person at the door continues to knock, teach your child to firmly say "we are not answering right now" through the closed door. Then immediately have them get on the phone and call you. If the person continues to stand at the front door, have your child call 911 and announce through the closed door that they have called the police. Children should not under any circumstances open the door until you, a trusted neighbor/friend or the police have arrived to help them.

<u>Notes for Parents:</u>
Make sure your child is mature enough and confident about being home alone before you decide to leave them alone. Review and practice emergency phone numbers and procedures often with your child before leaving them home alone. Identify trusted neighbors and friends your child can reach-out to in case they become scared or frightened. Keep a list of emergency numbers and contacts near the phone for your child. Ensure your child knows not to let anyone that calls or comes to the door that they are indeed home alone. Call and check-in with your child regularly.

Safety Topic: Water

What would you do if:
What would you do if a friend asked you to jump in the pool with them and no adults are present?

Questions:
1. What if you are a good swimmer?
2. What if you friend is an even better swimmer?
3. What if the friend's parents will be home soon?
4. What if you have a cell phone with you?
5. What if you friend reassures you that it is alright to swim without adults around?

Lessons your child should learn:
Children should never swim alone without adult supervision at the pool, lake or ocean. Even if your child is a very good swimmer, an adult or lifeguard needs to watch out for their safety while they are swimming. Explain that even exceptional swimmers have hit their head or lost their breath while swimming and needed help.

Notes for Parents:
According to Safe Kids USA, approximately 815 children between the ages of 1-14 drown each year in the United States. Enroll your child in swim lessons at any early age and set-up very firm rules about when and where they are allowed to swim. Teach your child

that a trusted adult or lifeguard always has to be "on watch" while they are swimming. When attending pool and lake parties, assign one or more adults or lifeguards to supervise the children <u>at all times</u>. Sadly, many drownings have occurred at parties in which many adults and kids were present, but no one adult was directly assigned to supervise the children.

Safety Topic: Fire

What would you do if:
What would you do if the smoke detector in your home begins to beep?

Questions:
1. What if you are sleeping in bed when you hear the noise?
2. What if your parents are home at the time?
3. What if your dog or cat is inside the home?
4. What if you smell smoke?
5. What if your parents are not at home?

Lessons your child should learn:
Teach your child to get out of the house immediately when there is a fire or smoke. Work with them to develop a family fire safety plan. The plan should include different routes to safety from every room in the home. Practice and review the plan often. The plan should include a meeting spot outside safely away from the home.

Notes for Parents:
The U.S. Fire Administration reports that more than 3,500 Americans die in fires each year, and approximately 18,300 are injured. Most of the fires occur in the home. Make sure you have working smoke alarms on every floor of your home. Teach your child that they are more valuable and precious than any other object

in the home. In the event of a fire, they should get out of the house as fast as they can! Review and practice possible escape routes to safety from all of the rooms in the house. Tell your child not to worry about personal belongings and pets. Ensure them that you will leave a door open for the family pet to escape if necessary.

Safety Topic: Bicycle

What would you do if:

What would you do if while riding bikes with friends they ask you to cross a busy highway with them?

Questions:

1. What if you are not wearing your bicycle helmet?
2. What if they tell you they cross this busy highway all the time?
3. What if there is not a bike lane or sidewalk you can ride on?
4. What if your parents do not know about these plans?
5. What if you cannot remember how to use proper hand turn signals for bike riding?
6. What if your friends tell you it is not "cool" to wear a bicycle helmet?

Lessons your child should learn:

Teach your child the importance of wearing a bicycle helmet to protect their head.

Work together with your child to develop a bicycle safety plan. Bicycle safety practices should include: stopping to check for traffic before riding into the street; learning how to properly and safely execute turns; ride with traffic instead of against it; and to obey traffic signs and lights. Review the rules often and set boundaries about where, when and with whom they are allowed to ride bikes.

Notes for Parents:

Practice safely crossing the road and biking on neighborhood streets with your child. Ensure your child stays alert and aware of oncoming vehicles and traffic. Dress your child in bright colors and a properly fitted helmet when they are biking. Teach and demonstrate how your child should safely navigate parked cars and driveways. Don't assume that neighborhood streets are bicycle-friendly. The most common crashes involve riding into the street without stopping, turning left or into oncoming traffic, running stop signs, and riding against the flow of traffic.

Safety Topic: Vehicle

What would you do if:
What would you do if you are riding in a car with a friend and they tell you that you don't have to wear a seat belt?

Questions:
1. What if the friend's mother is driving and tells you that you don't have to wear a seatbelt?
2. What if your friend tells you that it is not cool to wear a seatbelt?
3. What if you are riding with your mother and a bug lands on you?
4. What if you are in heavy traffic during a downpour?
5. What if you knew your mother was having a difficult time finding the destination?
6. What if you are afraid of bugs?
7. What if your sibling who is sitting next to you, just got into trouble for being too loud?

Lessons your child should learn:
Wear a seatbelt! This is **THE** most important thing you can do to protect yourself and your family. According to the National Highway Traffic Safety Administration, wearing lap/shoulder belts reduce the risk of a traffic fatality to front seat occupants by 45%!

Children also need to learn that it is important for the driver to stay alert and focused on driving safely. Your child and other children riding in the vehicle need to refrain from yelling, hitting, throwing objects or doing anything that will distract the driver. Set expectations on how your children should behave in the car and reinforce the rules often.

Notes for Parents:

Set a good example for your children by always buckling up EVERY time you get in your car. In most states, you can be pulled over and given a ticket if you are not buckled! According to AAA, Distracted driving contributes to approximately 8,000 crashes per day in the U.S. Passengers are the most frequently reported distraction with young children being four more times distracting than adults. Lead by example when you are driving by not using your mobile phone and remaining focused when behind the wheel.

Safety Topic: Dog Safety

What would you do if:
What would you do if your neighbor's dog escaped from the back yard and approached you?

Questions:
1. What if you like dogs?
2. What if this dog has previously barked at you?
3. What if you are afraid of dogs?
4. What if your neighbor said the dog was friendly?
5. What if you are wearing a winter coat?

Lessons your child should learn:
Children need to understand that some dogs may not like them or even like children, and may act aggressive towards them. Children should not approach unfamiliar dogs. Teach your child that if a dog approaches, chases or acts aggressive, to move away slowly to a safe place. They should not run, scream or make sudden movements that may further entice the dog to chase or bite them. If a dog is attacking and the child is knocked down, he/she should curl up in a ball and protect their head, face and neck. Demonstrate and practice this with your child.

Notes for Parents:

Over 4.5 million people are bitten by dogs each year. Among children, the highest rate of dog-bite related injuries is for ages 5 to 9. Teach your children not to pet or play with a dog that is eating, sleeping or caring for puppies. Show your child how to hold out their hand to allow a dog to "sniff" them before petting. Assume that stray dogs or dogs that are acting unusual are not safe, and report them to animal control. Do not bring a dog with a history of aggressive behavior into the home. Never leave infants or young children alone with a dog.

Safety Topic: Gun

What would you do if:
What would you do if you found a gun at the playground?

Questions:
1. What if there are not any adults around?
2. What if you have seen a similar gun like this on TV?
3. What if your brother or sister is with you?
4. What if your friends at school would like to see a gun?
5. What if you know the gun is not loaded – would you play with it?

Lessons your child should learn:
Children should never touch or play with guns. Teach them to make an immediate report to you or a trusted adult if they find themselves near or around a gun. Children and adults should always assume a gun is a loaded gun. Tell your child that firearms are capable of bodily injury, destruction and even death if misused. Be open and honest with your child about the dangers of guns.

Notes for Parents:
Approximately 500 children are shot by guns every year in the United States. If you have guns in the home, make sure all guns are safely stored in a lock box and that the ammunition is locked up in a separate lock box. Children are curious by nature, so it is extremely important to keep all guns and ammunition under lock and key.

Before your child goes to spend time at a friend's or relative's home, ask if there are guns in the home and if so, are they safely locked up? Education, responsibility and honesty are key components in preventing gun accidents. Teach your children about gun safety and the dangerous consequences. If you own guns, lead by example by properly handling them and responsibly storing them. Encourage your child to come and talk to you openly and honestly about anything anytime-even if they or a friend of theirs has made a mistake.

Safety Topic: What if you are lost?

What would you do if:
What would you do if you became lost from your parents at the mall?

Questions:
1. What if a mommy with kids asks if you need help?
2. What if you see an information booth nearby?
3. What if a man offers to take you outside of the mall to try and find them?
4. What if you see a security guard across the hall?
5. What if a store clerk who is standing behind a cash register asks you if you need help?

Lessons your child should learn:
If a child becomes lost from their parents or caregivers at a public place, they need to be able to identify those that can help them. A mommy or grandmother with kids, a police or security officer, a store clerk wearing a name badge, or employees at an information desk are all good choices. Teach your child to approach the mommy, police officer or clerk and tell them they are lost and need help. Instruct them to stay in the original location in which they became lost. They are not to go off with anyone and try to find you. Reassure them that you will not stop looking for them until they are found.

Notes for Parents:

According to the National Center for Missing and Exploited Children, nearly 800,000 children under the age of 18 are missing every year, or an average of 2,158 children reported missing every day. If your child is missing, act immediately and search for your child. If your child is lost in a public place or store, enlist the police, security or store employees to help you find your child.

Many stores participate in a lost child practice called "Code Adam" which is sponsored by the National Center for Missing and Exploited Children. The program trains store employees and managers to guard all exits until your child is found and the police arrive. Next time you are out shopping at your favorite retail store, ask the store manager if they participate in "Code Adam?"

Safety Topic: Internet Safety

What would you do if:

What would you do if you are on the computer and someone you do not know in "real life" sends you a message asking you your name, age and address?

Questions:

1. What if you had communicated with this person via the computer before?
2. What if this person told you personal information about themselves?
3. What if this person asks you to send a picture of yourself?
4. What if you would like for this person to be your friend?
5. What if some of your friends communicate via the computer with people they do not know in "real life?"

Lessons your child should learn:

Children should never give out their personal information including name, phone number, address, email address, and where they go to school or hang out over the internet. Explain to your child that it is not safe and could put them and the family at-risk. Children should not share personal information on the internet with people they do not know in "real life." Ask your child to alert you if someone they do not know tries to communicate with them on the internet. Reassure them that you will investigate the matter, and that they will not be punished for being honest and forthright. Encouraging open dialogue and discussion is a key element in keeping your kids safe online.

Notes for Parents:
A recent survey conducted by the National Center for Missing and Exploited Children indicates that nearly 30% of children ages 8-12 have been contacted by a stranger online. One in five tweens post personal information about themselves including photos, the city they live in, and their age. If your children use the internet, it is critical to protect their identity and guard their personal information.

Safety Topic: Social Media

What would you do if:
What would you do if a friend shared a picture of you on a social networking site without your permission?

Questions:
1. What if you do not want anyone to see the picture?
2. What if the picture provides details on where you go to school?
3. What if you also have a social networking account?
4. What if your friend does not meet the age requirements for social networking accounts?
5. What if you believe your parents would not like anyone to see this picture?

Lessons your child should learn:
Once something is posted on the internet it cannot be completely taken back. Discuss the implications of sharing personal photos and personal information on the Internet with your child. Teach your child to protect their identity and photos of themselves on the Internet. Children should communicate to their friends that they do not want pictures or personal information posted without their permission (and ultimately, yours).

<u>Notes for Parents:</u>
Both Facebook and Instagram require users to be at least 13 years old to have an account. Abiding by the age limits will help you safeguard your child from sharing too much personal information before they are mature enough to understand the ramifications. Promote computer safety in your house by having your child use the computer in an open room and regularly check-in on them.

Safety Topic: Drugs/Alcohol

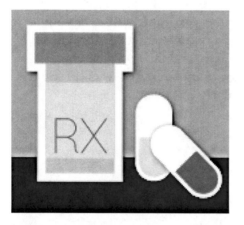

What would you do if:
What would you do if a friend asked you to try an illegal drug or alcohol?

Questions:
1. What if you are very close with this friend and trust them?
2. What if you are told the drug is harmless?
3. What if you are worried that if you do not try the drug/alcohol, your friend will not like you anymore?
4. What if you already know that drugs and alcohol can hurt you?
5. What if you are worried your parents will find out?
6. What are some things that can happen if you are caught with an illegal drug or with alcohol?

Lessons your child should learn:
Talk to your children about the dangers of illegal drugs and alcohol. Explain that there are some illegal drugs that can cause you to become addicted even if only tried one time. Further explain to your child that if a "friend" is asking them to try something that could damage their mind and body, then that person is not a "real friend" at all. Ask your children to come to you openly to discuss drugs and alcohol. Reassure them that you are always there for them no matter what.

<u>Notes for Parents:</u>

According to a 2012 survey conducted by The National Center on Addiction and Substance Abuse at Columbia University, 17% of high school students drink, smoke and use drugs during the school day. The survey found that 44% of the students know a classmate who is selling drugs at school, and 60% percent report that drugs are available on campus. Peer pressure and digital peer pressure definitely play a part in these staggering statistics as 75% of the students surveyed report that they are more likely to use drugs and alcohol if they see pictures of their friends using them. These statistics indicate that it is paramount for parents to encourage open dialogue and discussion in the home about drugs and alcohol, and engage in their children's lives.

SPECIAL BONUS CONTENT - EMPOWERING YOUR CHILD

The following **BONUS CONTENT** is a chapter written by Gary Martin Hays and Diena Thompson in the Best Selling book "The Success Secret: The World's Leading Experts Reveal Their Secret Secrets for Success in Business and in Life." Jack Canfield, the creator of the "Chicken Soup For The Soul" series, also contributed to the book. Since its release, it landed on Amazon.com's Best Seller's List and has received rave reviews, including testimonials from:

Elizabeth Smart, Abduction Survivor

" Too many families experience the nightmare of having a child go missing. I know what it is like to be that child. I know what it is like to think that one false move may lead to not only your own death but the death of family members as well. Nobody can ever blame a child for their actions when they are being threatened, bullied, forced, or coerced into doing something unthinkable. What if we could prevent future crimes against children? Wouldn't it be worth it to do everything to bring home that one child? **We do have options.** Gary and Diena have successfully written about the radKIDS program that was created not to react to a heinous crime committed against a child, but to prevent crimes from happening to children."

Ed Smart, Father of Elizabeth Smart

"As the father of a child that was abducted, I have a unique perspective and an intense passion to make certain that children have every tool they need to do everything they can to stay safe. I believe Gary and Diena have successfully outlined what every parent and child, and community should do to ensure all children go through the radKIDS program and develop their own tool kit on how to stay safe."

Steve Daley, Founder of radKIDS

"As a retired law enforcement professional and founder of the radKIDS Personal Empowerment Safety Education curriculum I would like to thank my friends and fellow advocates Gary Martin Hays and Diena Thompson for sharing a message from their hearts about the radKIDS Education Model. The time is now to take our children back from predatory violence in our society. As I learned in my law enforcement career the only way to stop a bad guy (predator) is to make them stop. radKIDS empowers our children to recognize,avoid, resist and, if necessary, make someone STOP! "Education is the only tool we have to take away fear and turn it into power." radKIDS is the foundation for a realistic safety education including a starting mindset of, "HOW DARE YOU instead of "Help me, Help Me, if and when anyone tries to hurt you." As children have told and taught me over the last 12 years, "Don't tell what to do to be safe, Teach me how to do it" radKIDS does just that. If you have a child, grandchild or just think the time has come to give children the power and skills they deserve to live safer in our world today I encourage you to start by reading this book to see, WHAT WE CAN DO instead of just hoping it does not happen. As always it is best said by a child who shared with their teacher at the end of his radKIDS class, " You know this stuff (radKIDS) is important I am with myself 24 hours a day" As Gary and Diena share, "Every kid should be a radKIDS." Read on and see why . . ."

Floy Turner, Special Agent – Florida Department of Law Enforcement (retired)

"After years of working on the Child Abduction Response Team as a Florida Department of Law Enforcement Special Agent and training thousands of law enforcement officers throughout the U. S. in responding to child abductions, I am convinced that focusing on preventative measures is often a neglected aspect of the overall child safety efforts. A few years ago, I was provided the opportunity to attend a radKIDS instructor training course. I feel that all children would benefit by learning the life saving skill sets provided through the successful and proven radKIDS program. This book provides the important message of being proactive and affording children with the ability to become empowered. On a personal note, my grandchildren are radKIDS!"

VI. Empowering Your Child: Why Every Kid Should be a radKID

"Safety and security don't just happen, they are the result of collective consensus and public investment. We owe our children, the most vulnerable citizens in our society, a life free of violence and fear."
—Nelson Mandela, former president of South Africa

The Tragic Story of Somer Thompson

At approximately 2:45 p.m. on October 19, 2009, seven-year-old Somer Thompson left her elementary school in Orange Park, Florida. She met up with her twin brother, Samuel, and their older sister, Abigail, for the mile walk home. Somer became separated from her siblings and she stopped to talk to Jarred Harrell, one of 161 registered sex offenders that lived within a five-mile radius of Somer's home. He lured Somer into his home to see his dog. Once she was inside, he raped and asphyxiated her.

When Somer did not make it home, an investigation was launched. The local Child Abduction Response Team (CART) was activated. This is a team of local and state law enforcement agencies with specialized training to respond to a missing or abducted child. Unfortunately, the search and recovery efforts were to no avail. Two days later, her body
was found when a garbage truck that carried a load of trash from her neighborhood spilled its load in a Georgia landfill nearly 50 miles away.

On February 3, 2012, Harrell entered a plea of guilty and agreed not to appeal any of his convictions to avoid the death penalty. He was sentenced to life in prison with no possibility of parole. At the sentencing hearing, Somer's twin brother, Samuel, told Harrell from the witness stand "[Y]ou know you did this, and now you are going to jail."

Diena Thompson

Diena Thompson is the surviving mother of Somer. Having your child abducted is certainly a parent's worst nightmare, and it unfortunately came true for Diena. As a surviving parent, no one could blame her if she chose to deal with this horrific tragedy in private. Yet, Diena has taken the opposite approach and has made it her life's mission to make sure no other parent has to suffer. She formed The Somer Thompson Foundation in 2010 with the purpose to "provide education in the form of awareness and prevention to both parents and children to avoid the tragedy of experiencing the loss of a child." Diena believes every child should have the opportunity to be a radKID.

What Can We Do To Prevent This Tragedy From Ever Happening Again?

There are countless books available to adults on so many subjects involving self-improvement—everything from how to be a better communicator to how to be more confident, whether we are speaking to one person or an audience of thousands. The other chapters in this book all deal with "Success Secrets" we, as adults, can use to help us achieve greater success in life. But there are few books or other resources writ- ten specifically with children in mind. What can we as parents do to help insure our child's success in life?

We need to empower our children to be able to stand up for themselves and to be able to protect themselves.

We want to be with our children 24/7. We want to put them in protective headgear and bubble wrap every time they walk out the door. But author Anne Cassidy writes in her book, *Parents Who Think Too Much*, "[T]he suits of armor we provide them are as dangerous as the world we're protecting them from." We cannot become so obsessed with our children's safety that our worry becomes debilitating paranoia.

Are there reasons we should be concerned about our children's safety? Let's debunk some common misconceptions:

- *"These 'predators' do not live in my neighborhood."* The U.S. Department of Justice estimates there is one registered sex offender per square mile in the United States.

- *"My children are too young to be exposed to threats from sexual predators."* The average age at which sexual abuse begins is 3 years old. 1 of every 3 reports of sexual abuse to law enforcement are children under 12 years of age. 1 of every 7 are under age 6.
- *"My child would never fall for the lost puppy trick."* 85% of the time a child is abducted it involves the use of physical force where the predator grabs the child.
- *"I never leave my child alone with strangers."* 90% of sexual assault/abuse victims knew their offender. 59% were within the family; 37% were acquaintances of the victim or the victim's family.

What are the success principles we need to give to our children? What can we do to prepare our children to strike back against what Stephen M. Daley, M.Ed., the founder and executive director of radKIDS, calls the "ABC'S of Child Victimization"?
Abduction
Bullying
Child abuse and Neglect
Sexual Assault

radKIDS
We think the best program available to our children is **radKIDS,** the national leader in children's safety education. Stephen Daley left law enforcement after a distinguished 20-year career. Since starting radKIDS, he has trained and certified over 4,000 instructors across the nation.
The "rad" in radKIDS stands for "Resisting Aggression Defensively." Or as Daley likes to put it in children's terms: "**A radKID is a cool kid who doesn't let anyone hurt them**."
radKIDS is making a difference. More than 250,000 children have been trained in the program. More than 80 children threatened with abduction have used their radKIDS skills and returned safely to their families. There have been over 5,000 documented disclosures of sexual abuse, and the program has empowered these children to speak up and get the help they needed to stop the violence in their lives.

radKIDS has 3 guiding principles for all kids, and we believe these are three "SUCCESS PRINCIPLES" every child should learn. Please understand - these are merely words. When coupled with the addition of realistic physical resistance to violence skills (hands-on drills) that train the brain to react - this radKIDS program empowers the child - and gives them the ability and potential to never be a victim.

radKIDS Rule #1: No One Has The Right To Hurt Me Because I Am Special.

Children need to know they "matter." All human beings have this inherent desire, as it is a key to our existence, just as important as air, food and water. We need to guide our kids in a direction that they know, feel and believe that they are important—to us as parents, and to themselves. If a child has a healthy self-esteem, they are better prepared to address all of the challenges they are going to face in this world. If they feel good about themselves—if they know they are special—they will have an easier time handling conflicts and issues as they arise, will resist negative peer pressure, and will stand up for themselves if anyone tries to hurt them.

This feeling of self-value, self worth is also critical in teaching the child that he or she does not have the right to hurt him or herself. Why? Because they are special. This is extremely important when dealing with issues such as drug or alcohol abuse. "You should not try cocaine or crystal meth as you will be hurting yourself" and "No one has the right to hurt me—including myself—because I am special."

Further, kids with a healthy self-esteem enjoy interacting with others, are comfortable in social settings, yet feel capable of working independently. They are not intimidated by challenges and can work towards solutions. These children do not give up easily nor wait for someone to step in to help.

When confronted by a predator and grabbed, a radKID is trained to react and is empowered to protect themselves. The radKID learns to replace the fear, confusion, and panic of a dangerous situation with confidence, personal safety skills, and self-esteem. When grabbed, a radKID thinks and says "How dare you touch me" versus "Help me, help me."

Here are some tips parents can use to help build healthy self-esteem in our children:

- Show consistent love and affection to your child: Hugs and spontaneous affection are great boosters.
- Compliment your child! Mothers were asked in a survey to keep track of how many times they made negative comments versus positive comments to their children. They admitted that the ratio was 10 negative comments to only 1 positive comment. A three year survey in one city's school found that the teachers' comments were 75% negative. In addition, it takes four (4) positive statements to offset the effects of one negative statement to a child. Institute of Family Relations in *Homemade*, December 1986.
- Be proud of your child and talk positively about your child! Tell him or her how proud you are to be their parent! And let them hear you speak positively about them to your friends and to theirs.
- Be a Role Model! Lead by example. Do not be excessively harsh on yourself, or have a negative attitude all of the time. Nurture your own self-esteem, and give your child a positive image to mirror.

radKIDS Rule #2: I Don't Have The Right To Hurt Anyone Else Unless They Are Trying To Hurt Me and Then I Have Every Right To Stop Them.

Some parents and educators immediately hear about radKIDS and think "This program is teaching kids how to fight." Nothing could be further from the truth. When children go through the course, they are taught the rules of context; i.e., when the use of physical resistance is appropriate, and when it is not. As Daley points out, "They must understand that their responses must be in proportion to the aggression they are facing. We don't want our students to use excessive force when it is not war- ranted, nor do we want them to be afraid to physically resist when they are in real jeopardy."

He refers to these as the "When you can and When You can't" rules. In a situation where the child is being teased or threatened with harm or physical violence, radKIDS are taught:

- If it's someone you know, leave immediately and advise a parent.
- If it's someone you don't know, run to escape.
- If you cannot run, PEPPER, HAMMER, KICK to escape. (These are defense skills taught to students).
- Use your radKIDS skills to avoid being carried off or dragged into a vehicle.
- In radKIDS, Physical Resistance means stopping someone from hurting you):

YELL LOUD! HIT HARD! RUN FAST!
(All taught defensively)

Think about Rule #2 for a moment and its application to the problem of bullying in our schools. Bullying happens when someone tries to hurt others by:

- Making them feel threatened
- Hurting them by kicking, hitting, pushing, tripping
- Name-calling
- Spreading nasty rumors

The person that is being bullied often times feels helpless, like he or she can't do anything to stop it. The victims of bullying, the children most prone to being picked on, tend to have the following characteristics:

- Low self-esteem (remember radKIDS rule #1!)
- Insecure
- Lack social skills
- Cry or become emotionally distraught easily
- Unable to defend or stand up for themselves

Here are some disturbing statistics on bullying: Every 7 minutes a child is bullied. In those situations, an adult only intervened in 4% of them. 85% of the time, there was no intervention on behalf of the child being bullied by anyone—adults, friends, or other children.

- 90% of all students in grades 4-8 reported being threatened and bullied in school.
- About 22% of students in grades 4-8 reported academic difficulties as a result of bullying.
- 864,000 students report staying home at least one day a month because they fear for their safety in school.

Too many schools have employed a "Zero Tolerance" rule when dealing with bullying. "Zero tolerance" means that any violation of the rules, no matter how minuscule or what the circumstances, will be punished severely. The aggressor and the person being attacked - if they fight back - are punished the same way. It is more of a political response than an educationally sound solution. It sounds impressive for school officials to say that we are taking a tough stand on bullying. "Zero tolerance" makes "Zero sense." Empowering children can, and will, create a partnership and a more powerful learning climate and culture in our schools, one founded on a "Zero Victimization" environment where everyone knows "No one" gets hurt here.

Steve Daley often asks this rhetorical question: "How many times should your child's head be slammed against the bathroom floor at school before you allow him the opportunity to strike back, or while he waits for an adult to intervene?"

It defies common sense to punish a child for trying to protect him or herself when being attacked. Recent studies by the federal government find that prevention programs that focus on changing the overall school culture, by taking such steps as having the entire student body involved in bully prevention, are better at reducing school violence. radKIDS changes the culture of the school—not from the top down—but from *within* the student body when the kids realize they are all subject to the 3 radKIDS Rules.

radKIDS Rule #3: If Anyone Tries To Hurt Me, Trick Me, or Make Me Feel Bad Inside or Out, It's Not My Fault — So I Can Tell.

So many kids need to hear those words, especially in the case of sexual abuse. Sherryl Kraizer, Ph.D., writes in *The Safe Child Book*, "[O]ne of the most important elements in a child's recovery is the placing of responsibility where it lies—with the perpetrator." A professional trained in counseling children who are victims in abuse can help the child understand that what happened to them was not their fault, and they did not do anything wrong.

Children also need to know if they are being bulled, abused, or are threatened in any way, it is okay to tell you. radKIDS also adds this advice. "It's important to let your child know they can tell you anything. But also tell them if you get mad or upset, you are not mad at them, but you are angry at the person who hurt them." You don't want your child shutting down the dialogue with you because they feel they have disappointed you or hurt you in some way.

In cases of sexual abuse, children are very hesitant to tell their parents what has happened for several reasons, including:

- Fear of what may happen to them
- Fear of what may happen to the abuser
- Fear of disappointment for their parents
- Fear they will not be believed

If children are not empowered to tell, then parents can look for some nonverbal signs that abuse may be occurring, including:

- The child does not want to be alone with someone known to them or the family
- Sleep difficulties and nightmares
- Acting out or experiencing problems at school
- Using sexual terms or explicit names for body parts
- Displaying inappropriate physical affection

And thanks to radKIDS, thousands of empowered children have

spoken up and received the help the needed to stop the abuse in their lives.

So What Happens now?

So what can you do to help empower your children or the children in your life? Together, we can make a difference One Child and One Com- munity at a Time. The long-term, lasting solution is to have the radKIDS curriculum incorporated into the elementary school's physical education department. It meets curriculum and education standards in all 50 states. As Diena likes to say, "Every child deserves an opportunity to feel safe and be safer in their world today. Is it not our children's right to this type of education and empowerment and, in fact, our responsibility as parents, educators and citizens to make it happen? Together, we can make sure EVERY child becomes empowered through radKIDS and it will help break the potential cycle of violence in our children's lives, and therefore, in all our futures." Bring radKIDS to your community by getting yourself trained as an instructor. You can teach the course after school or during the summer. To learn more about this personal empowerment safety education program, please visit www.radKIDS.org.

VII. Let's Protect Our Kids

Two final things we want to stress to everyone that reads this book:

(1) This book is just a starting point for you to openly discuss safety issues with your child or children. We want this to be the beginning of a dialogue, and hopefully a springboard for you to find a class in your area that effectively reinforces these safety concepts through skills and drills. Find a course that uses all three of the ways of learning – auditory, visual and kinesthetic – to try and ensure their reactions to dangerous situations becomes second nature. Please refer back to the "WARNING" section of this book to learn more about how Behavioral Skills Training (BST).

(2) THANK YOU!!!

All proceeds from the sale of this book will go to benefit "Let's Protect Our Kids", a program of Keep Georgia Safe.org, a 501(c)(3) charitable organization with the mission to provide safety education and crime prevention training to our families. Your purchase of this book allows us to educate more families on how to be safe, as well as to fund the training of more police officers in Child Abduction Response Team, or CART. We sincerely thank you for your generosity, and for taking that affirmative step to protect your family and yourself!

To find out more, visit www.KeepGeorgiaSafe.org.

Notes

Important Warning

1. (*Teaching Students to Read Through Their Individual Learning Styles*, Marie Carbo, Rita Dunn, and Kenneth Dunn; Prentice-Hall, 1986, p. 13).
2. Gunby, Kristin V., Carr, James E. and Leblanc, Linda A. "Teaching Abduction-Prevention Skills To Children With Autism", Journal Of Applied Behavior Analysis 43, Number 1 (Spring 2010), pp. 107-112.
3. (Dancho, K.A., Thompson, R.H., and Rhoades, M.M. (2008). Teaching preschool children to avoid poison hazards. Journal of Applied Behavior Analysis, 41, 287-271.
4. (Himle, M.D., Miltenberger, R.G., Flessner, C., and Gatheridge, B. (2004) Teaching safety skills to children to prevent gun play. Journal of Applied Behavior Analysis, 37. 1-9.
5. (Johnson, B.M., Miltenberger, R.G., Knudson, P., Egemo-Helm, K., Jostad, C.M., Flessner, C., & Gatheridge, B. (2005). Evaluation of behavioral skills training for teaching abduction-prevention skills to young children. Journal of Applied Behavior Analysis, 38, 67-78.

Introduction

1. De Becker, Gavin. *Protecting The Gift*. New York: Dell Publishing, 1999.
2. www.missingkids.com/en_US/documents/homicide_missing. pdf.
3. Debra Boyer and David Fine. "Sexual Abuse as a Factor in Adolescent Pregnancy and Child Maltreatment." Family Planning Perspectives, vol. 24, no. 1, Jan. 1992.
4. Lieb, R., Quinsey, V., and Berliner, L., "Sexual Predators and Social Policy," in M. Tonry (Ed), Crime and Justice (University of Chicago, 1998): 43-114.

5. Christensen, Kim, and Felch, Jason. "Boy Scouts help alleged molesters cover tracks, files show". *Los Angeles Times*, 16 September 2012. Local. Print.
6. Cassidy, Anne. *Parents Who Think Too Much*. New York: Dell Publishing, 1998.

Safety Scenarios

1. Daley, Stephen, *radKIDS Personal Empowerment Safety Education Curriculum*, 2001.
2. Daley, Stephen, *radKIDS Personal Empowerment Safety Education Curriculum*, 2001.
3. Daley, Stephen, *radKIDS Personal Empowerment Safety Education Curriculum*, 2001.
4. Daley, Stephen, *radKIDS Personal Empowerment Safety Education Curriculum*, 2001.
5. Daley, Stephen, *radKIDS Personal Empowerment Safety Education Curriculum*, 2001.

About The Authors

About Gary

Gary Martin Hays is not only a successful lawyer, but is a nationally recognized safety advocate who works tirelessly to educate our families and children on issues ranging from bullying to internet safety to abduction prevention. He currently serves on the Board of Directors of the Elizabeth Smart Foundation. Gary has been seen on countless television stations, including CNN's Headline News, ABC, CBS, NBC and FOX affiliates. He has appeared on over 110 radio stations, including the Georgia News Network, discussing legal topics and providing safety tips to families. He hosts "Georgia Behind The Scenes" on the CW Atlanta TV Network and has been quoted in *USA Today, The Wall Street Journal,* and featured on over 250 online sites including *Yahoo News, Morningstar.com, CBS News' MoneyWatch.com, the Boston Globe, The New York Daily News and The Miami Herald.*

He is also co-author of the best-selling books "TRENDSETTERS - The World's Leading Experts Reveal Top Trends To Help You Achieve Health, Wealth and Success," "CHAMPIONS - Knockout Strategies For Health, Wealth and Success," "SOLD - The World's Leading Real Estate Experts Reveal The Secrets To Selling Your Home For Top Dollar In Record Time," "Protect And Defend," "The Success Secret: The World's Leading Experts Reveal Their Secrets for Success in Business and in Life," and "The Authority on Tout: How to Use Social Media's Newest Video Sharing App to Engage Your Community and Grow Your Business." In 2012, he was inducted into the National Academy of Best Selling Authors.

Gary graduated from Emory University in 1986 with a B.A. degree in Political Science and a minor in Afro-American and African Studies. In 1989, he received his law degree from the Walter F. George School of Law of Mercer University, Macon, Georgia. His outstanding academic achievements landed him a position on Mercer's Law Review. He also served the school as Vice President of the Student Bar Association.

His legal accomplishments include being a member of the prestigious Multi Million Dollar Advocate's Forum, a society limited to those attorneys who have received a settlement or verdict of at least $2 Million Dollars. He has been recognized in Atlanta Magazine as one of Georgia's top workers' compensation lawyers. Gary frequently lectures to other attorneys in Georgia on continuing education topics. He has been recognized as one of the Top 100 Trial Lawyers in Georgia since 2007 by the American Trial Lawyers Association, and recognized by Lawdragon as one of the leading Plaintiffs' Lawyers in America. His firm specializes in personal injury, wrongful death, workers' compensation, and pharmaceutical claims. Since 1993, his firm has helped over 27,000 victims and their families recover over $235 Million dollars.

In 2008, Gary started the non-profit organization Keep Georgia Safe with the mission to provide safety education and crime prevention training in Georgia. Keep Georgia Safe has trained over 80 state and local law enforcement officers in CART (Child Abduction Response Teams) so our first responders will know what to do in the event a child is abducted in Georgia. Gary has completed Child Abduction Response Team training with the National AMBER Alert program through the U.S. Department of Justice and Fox Valley Technical College. He is a certified instructor in the radKIDS curriculum. His law firm has given away 1,000 bicycle helmets and 14 college scholarships.

About Adam

Starting with a BS in Industrial Design and a Certificate in Marketing from Georgia Tech, Adam Weart has spent the past decade providing unmatched design and services to clients, specializing in corporate branding, social media and web design.

Adam spent four years running Design and Engineering for HomeWaves while leading the initiative for branding, marketing and sales. During his leadership, HomeWaves achieved their industry's most prestigious recognition by receiving 3 National CEDIA Awards.

He also co-authored the best-selling books, "CHAMPIONS - Knockout Strategies For Health, Wealth and Success" and "The Authority on Tout: How to Use Social Media's Newest Video Sharing App to Engage Your Community and Grow Your Business," and has been featured on *Yahoo News, CBS News' Moneywatch.com, The Miami Herlad* and *the San Francisco Chronicle.*

Adam continues to extend his leadership and marketing creativity by leveraging all aspects of Social Media Marketing and Web Usability Design as a key leader at the Law Offices of Gary Martin Hays & Associates, P.C.

About Mary Ellen

A background in education and child protection instruction fully prepared Mary Ellen Fulkus for her post as Executive Director of Keep Georgia Safe, where she oversees all safety curriculum development and program implementation, community and media awareness. She also works as an Independent Consultant within the Criminal Justice Services Child Protection Training for Fox Valley Technical College, a U.S. Department of Justice initiative. Mary Ellen is founder of The Safe-T-Net, Inc. a safety and security training and consulting company for schools, businesses, adults and children.

In March of 2007, Mary Ellen participated in the CART (Child Abduction Response Team) AMBER Alert Training Conference in Houston, Texas. She is a nationally-certified r.a.d. (Resisting Aggression Defensively) KIDS Instructor and a participant in the Florida Department of Law Enforcement Training Conference on Crimes Against Children, in Pensacola, Florida.

A former 8th grade teacher, Mary Ellen completed a Graduate Leadership Certification Program in Public School Administration at The University of Georgia in 2004. She also earned a master's degree in education from Mercer University in Atlanta, and received her undergraduate degree from Florida State University.

To find out more about Mary Ellen Fulkus and Keep Georgia Safe, please visit http://www.KeepGeorgiaSafe.org or call (770) 934-8000.

CPSIA information can be obtained at www.ICGtesting.com
Printed in the USA
LVOW09s0335291014

410872LV00005B/759/P